Do not be anxious about anything, but in every situation, by prayer and petition, with thanksgiving, present your requests to God. And the peace of God, which transcends all understanding, will guard your hearts and your minds in Christ Jesus.

Philippians 4:6–7 NIV

40 Prayers for My Wife

Drawing near to God for the woman you love.

by Ryan Frederick

40 Prayers for My Wife

Drawing near to God for the woman you love.

Published by Cormens Press, a division of Vilicus LLC

First Edition

ISBN-10: 0-9974713-4-4

ISBN-13: 978-0-9974713-4-2

(pbk. bw.)

1 3 5 7 9 10 8 6 4 2 22 21 20 19 18

Printed in the United States of America

To Luke Wilbanks,
friend, brother, and man of prayer

Contents

Introduction

Writing this book changed me, and I'm hoping it can do the same for you.

Prayer is one of those things we take for granted. Personally, it's a concept I rarely think twice about. It almost feels common . . . normal. Maybe even a bit cliché. But if you stop and think about it, prayer shouldn't seem normal. It shouldn't seem commonplace. It should seem more crazy than normal—outlandish, even.

Is it ordinary for a man to converse with, listen to, and commune with the living God of the universe? Is it normal for a finite person to have consistent dialogue with the all-powerful, all-knowing, and all-present Creator of everything?

There's no way prayer can be normal, is there? I didn't believe it could be for an imperfect, finite man. I'm the opposite of everything God is:

He is holy—perfect in every conceivable way—and I am not.

He is powerful beyond bounds; I'm painfully limited.

He is spirit; I am flesh and bone.

He exists forever without beginning or end, and I'm just trying not to die before I turn eighty.

In fact, the more I contemplate the vast chasm separating God and me, the further I plunge into an existential crisis. God is God, and I am not. It's that simple, and it's a reality I'll quickly accept. So, how could I ever hope to know him and talk to him, let alone spend time communing with him?

Prayer, I've learned is a prime example of how the upside-down, nonsensical, irrational grace of God shatters reality.

I don't have to be big enough or good enough to know God or spend time with him in his presence because of this one profound truth: Jesus is. Jesus is big enough and good enough. He made communion with God possible.

Now prayer doesn't feel so ridiculous. I can cross the chasm carried on Christ's back. I stand protected and justified, clothed in Jesus' righteousness instead of my own. I can boldly approach God's throne of grace without fear of being annihilated by his sheer, unfiltered glory.

Not only has writing this book convinced me that prayer—the act of communicating and communing with God himself—is possible, but the experience has also shown me that prayer is one of the most profound, necessary, and in fact, normal activities of my very existence as a disciple of Christ. I must pray as I must breathe. The wonder lies in the fact that I am able to pray just as I am able to breathe: solely because God ordains it.

The miracle doesn't end there. We aren't just warranted to enter into communion with God; we are also *wanted.* It's worth mentioning here because I feel like it's common to forget.

You are *wanted* by God.

Your prayers don't inconvenience him or challenge his patience. Nor do your prayers ever reach beyond his expectation or ability to answer. Instead, he listens eagerly. He stands ready, willing, and glad to hear—and answer—your prayers just as a loving father awaits the voice of his child. There's a reason Jesus taught his disciples (which includes you and me) to pray by starting with "Our Father"; our King knows us well, and he knew we'd need constant reminding that God is our loving Father, eager and glad to hear our prayers.

So, this is the primary way writing this book has changed me, and it's the single most important premise I urge you to remember over the next forty days: understand that God warrants *and* wants to hear your prayers because of Jesus, not you. Knowing you're wanted and welcomed into communion with God because Jesus made it possible provides the backdrop for a faith-filled, obedient, and expectant prayer life. After all, if we're going to be so gutsy as to directly approach the God of the universe, is there any other way we should dare to pray?

Jesus makes approaching God possible, but he didn't just open the door and leave us to fend for ourselves. He also gave us clear instruction for how to pray via the Lord's Prayer in Matthew 6. There are volumes upon volumes of books dedicated to this one prayer, so I'll leave in-depth, granular explanations to smarter men than me. While the prayers in this book don't strictly adhere to the structure of the Lord's Prayer, they do loosely follow its well-known A.C.T.S. progression: adoration, confession, thanksgiving, and finally, supplication.

I made an intentional decision not to adhere too strictly to a particular formula with each prayer for the sake of our theme: praying for your bride and the health of your marriage. For that reason, I highly recommend that this book function as a *supplement* to your own prayer and devotional routines. It's a tool to stir your heart and spur your mind toward articulating your personal thoughts unto God as they relate to your wife.

Three Encouragements

There are many ways I desire to encourage you as you begin this book, but for the sake of brevity I will keep it to three.

First, as you journey onward, I encourage you to be *hopeful*. Lean into the bigness and goodness of God as you contend for your wife. Get carried away as you imagine what God can do in and through your relationship. Let God be God, and be expectant of all he can do. Whatever change you're hoping to see over the next forty days, place it in his capable hands and watch as he works.

Next, I encourage you to *create margin* in your schedule. Prayer is a dialogue, and good dialogue takes time. You will notice a number of scripture references throughout each prayer. This is based on the idea that prayer is, in large part, a response to what God has already said in his Word. Pray with Scripture as the backbone of all you say, wrestle with it, and then let it breathe. In other words, God has spoken, the initial prayer is your response, and your final rest (silence) is time for the Holy Spirit to minister to you. While rushing through each prayer is better than no prayer at all, giving yourself an extra five to ten minutes to sit, wait, and listen will ensure you learn to hear your Father's voice well.

Finally, I encourage you to *pray continually*—not just throughout each day, but for the intended duration of the book. Here's what I mean: determine now to finish this book and spend five to fifteen minutes in it each day. Doing so will help you create a lasting prayer habit. Which leads me to my next point.

Why 40 Days?

The main reason we chose a 40-day duration was the hope that it would help you establish a new, lasting habit of prayer. Research shows that it takes between four and eight weeks to create a new habit. And of course, the longer you do something, the stronger the habit becomes.

On a different note, there's just something special about our chosen duration. The number 40 is a theme seen throughout the Bible. Moses was on Mount Sinai for 40 days and 40 nights (Exodus 24:18), Jesus spent 40 days and 40 nights in the desert, being tested (Matthew 4:2), there were 40 days between Jesus' resurrection and ascension (Acts 1:3), and a number of other occurrences of 40 as well.

We don't intend to place too much emphasis on some hidden meaning or secret to be unlocked by the number 40. It's not magical or mystical. However, we do see it as a sweet reminder of God's grace and sovereignty, which can be seen in the biblical passages and events where the number happens to be included.

To make things flexible, every seventh day is designated as an intentional rest day. Use it at your discretion. Feel free to catch up on missed days, journal, or spend extra time with your bride—it's your call. I do recommend silently reflecting on the chosen verse for a few minutes and jotting down anything that comes to mind. You will never regret it.

This is a book of prewritten prayers but it's more than just a compilation of scripts. It's a book about learning to go to God and trust him with your most precious human relationship. It's a book about believing Jesus is who the Bible says he is. It's a book about learning how to petition your loving Father boldly in light of his grace, on behalf of your wife.

If you're like me, you probably struggle to maintain a consistent habit of prayer. I'm thrilled to report that while I'm still imperfect, writing this book opened my eyes to the wonder and blessing it is to be able to petition God. It was *that* sense of wonder and *that* feeling of blessing that compelled me toward the more consistent prayer life I always wanted—and could've never mustered on my own.

I pray that as you embark on this forty-day prayer journey you will experience communion with God in deep new ways, and from there, that you will establish the beginnings of a lifelong, thriving prayer relationship with him.

Father, you are forever faithful. Thank you for the husband holding this book. I pray that you'd flood his heart and mind with your goodness, grace, and mercy. Use the next forty days for his good and your glory. Open his eyes to the wonder, power, and privilege of speaking with you as he contends for his wife. I pray that you'd cause his marriage to flourish from the inside out as you continue to transform his mind and mold him into the image of your Son. May your will be done over the coming days and weeks.

In Jesus' name, amen.

Taking Inventory

Every journey must have a destination in mind, but to know that, you must also know your starting point. Answer the questions below as honestly and specifically as you can. Then, watch and see what God does.

List some ways you have prayed for your wife currently or in the past.

What's on your wife's heart right now that you could pray for?

How would you like to grow in praying for your wife?

What difference do you think it could make in your marriage if you and your wife prayed for each other daily?

How are you praying God will move in your life and in your marriage over the next forty days? Be specific.

On a scale of 1 to 10, how would you rate the following areas of your marriage? (1 = Terrible, 10 = Great)

Overall Marital Unity, Health, and Enjoyment

1 2 3 4 5 6 7 8 9 10

Communication

1 2 3 4 5 6 7 8 9 10

Handling Conflict

1 2 3 4 5 6 7 8 9 10

Emotional Intimacy

1 2 3 4 5 6 7 8 9 10

Sexual Intimacy

1 2 3 4 5 6 7 8 9 10

Unity in Finances

1 2 3 4 5 6 7 8 9 10

Heads up: *At the end of the book, you will be prompted to return to this page and revisit your ratings above. At that time, circle your new numbers with a different-colored ink to get an idea of how God has worked in your marriage over the course of your 40-day journey.*

Remember the Whole Way

And you shall
remember the whole way
that the LORD your God has led
you these forty years in the
wilderness.

Deuteronomy 8:2

As you venture forth, use this area to quickly jot down instances when God answers prayer. Include dates and details. Refer back to it often to remind yourself of God's faithfulness.

Day 1

That She Would Be Good Soil

Hear then the parable of the sower: When anyone hears the word of the kingdom and does not understand it, the evil one comes and snatches away what has been sown in his heart. . . .

As for what was sown on good soil, this is the one who hears the word and understands it. He indeed bears fruit and yields, in one case a hundredfold, in another sixty, and in another thirty.

Matthew 13:18–19, 23

Father, thank you for your Word and its power to change hearts. You have lovingly instructed us and given us the unparalleled gift of letting us hear your will. Thank you for speaking clearly and decisively to us, and for making your voice clear in Scripture. I ask that you help my wife to be the good soil that Jesus spoke about in Matthew 13. Guard her heart from hardness, root her deeply in your Word, and protect her from worldly cares that would stifle the gospel's fruitfulness in her life. Give her ears to hear and eyes to see your truth (Matthew 11:15). May she be enlivened, encouraged, and emboldened when she reads Scripture. May the gospel bear fruit in her heart, and may its goodness overflow into every person she talks to throughout her day.

She works exceedingly hard in all she does; be her source of strength. Holy Spirit, remind her of her worth in you, and fill her with profound, endless joy (Psalm 16:11). Thank you for the woman she already is and the woman she's becoming. And thank you that I get to watch as you complete your work in her heart! You have commissioned me, as her husband, to play a role in helping her become the person you've created her to be. Give me wisdom to encourage her in the ways she needs most, and help me love her intentionally—how you would want your daughter to be loved.

Father, keep my wife's heart soft and attentive to your voice. I pray that whenever she reads or hears your Word, it would bear fruit. Multiply its yield a hundredfold in her life. Form her, mold her, and shape her into the woman you want her to be. And graciously use me—her husband—in that process however you see fit.

In Jesus' name, amen.

Use these pages to journal your thoughts, write your own prayer, or both.

Date ________________

Day 2
For Wisdom Beyond Her Years

Blessed is the one who finds wisdom, and the one who gets understanding, for the gain from her is better than gain from silver and her profit better than gold.

Proverbs 3:13–14

Father, by wisdom you founded the earth and by understanding you established the heavens (Proverbs 3:19). You truly are a masterful creator, and your work is unmatched! You instruct us in your Word to find wisdom because it's more valuable than anything else on the planet. I ask that you fill my wife's heart and mind with your wisdom. Give her understanding beyond her years and faith to believe what you say with depth and sincerity. I pray that when she reads your Word, it would saturate her heart with the truth and knowledge of you.

With wisdom deeply rooted in her heart, help my wife apply it diligently to every area of life. When she goes to work, let understanding govern her decisions. When she speaks to friends and family, may your wisdom guide everything she says. This world is filled with meaningless, idle words, complaints, and gossip. I pray that my wife sees empty words and chatter for what they are: foolishness. Give her wisdom to identify when conversations aren't glorifying to you, and grant her understanding to steer them another way. If she's powerless to change the circumstances, give her the courage to leave the conversation graciously but boldly.

Finally, I pray that my bride finds your knowledge to be a source of constant joy, delight, and encouragement. May the pleasantness and peace of your wisdom overrun her when she needs it most. Thank you for my wife—she is a gift and a treasure!

In Jesus' name, amen.

Use these pages to journal your thoughts, write your own prayer, or both.

Date ____________________

Day 3
Shield Her from Spiritual Attacks

Finally, be strong in the Lord and in the strength of his might. Put on the whole armor of God, that you may be able to stand against the schemes of the devil. For we do not wrestle against flesh and blood, but against the rulers, against the authorities, against the cosmic powers over this present darkness, against the spiritual forces of evil in the heavenly places.

Ephesians 6:10–12

God, if I stop and think about "spiritual forces" and "cosmic powers" that are warring against me, I usually have one of two reactions: fear or disbelief. Help me to understand this unseen war we are engaged in with accuracy and perspective; then give me faith to fight it as I am called. I realize that much of the daily battle we fight is against our own flesh (our sin nature), but there is another battlefront: the schemes of the devil. Grant my wife and me a firm understanding of both battlefronts, and help us to wage war with boldness, faith, and perseverance.

Lord, shield my wife from spiritual attacks. Help her to be strong in you, just as Paul instructed the Ephesians. You are our ultimate assurance, Jesus: your work, your power, and your name. There is no other name by which we are saved (Acts 4:12).

Help my wife to put her full trust in you if and when she feels tempted, afraid, attacked, or vulnerable. Give her supernatural boldness that is based on who you are and who you say she is. Give her strength to withstand every temptation and attack. She is your precious daughter, and you will protect her more than I ever could, but use me to lead and protect her however you wish.

Gird us with your armor and arm us with your weapons as we wage spiritual war. Protect our marriage from all manner of spiritual attack, and help us to fight with unity. God, we'd be helpless without you, but with you our victory is secure (1 Corinthians 15:57). Thank you for your covering, and for allowing us to seek shelter in the shadow of your wings (Psalm 17:8). I love you, I worship you, and I thank you for my wife today.

In Jesus' name, amen.

Use these pages to journal your thoughts, write your own prayer, or both.

Date ______________

Day 4
Grant Her Contentment

Keep your life free from love of money, and be content with what you have, for he has said, "I will never leave you nor forsake you." So we can confidently say, "The Lord is my helper; I will not fear; what can man do to me?"

Hebrews 13:5–6

Lord, you have given us all we need for life and godliness (2 Peter 1:3). Help me to never lose sight of that truth! Too often, I forget that you, the Creator of the universe, have called me by name and adopted me into your royal family and called me yours (Romans 8:14–17). That eternal fact alone should be enough to deter me from earthly despair and joy-stealing desire, yet I often lose perspective. Thank you for pursuing me and giving me all I need in Christ; please grant me eyes to see you clearly and give me grace to lead my wife in being content in you just as you are leading me to be the same.

Thank you for giving me the exact wife I needed. She is your grandest gesture of kindness to me, aside from my salvation. Thank you for her faithfulness in how she follows you. Enrich her walk with you, Jesus. Call her into a deeper place of joy with you. Lord, protect her heart from every discontentment that isn't somehow rooted in your gospel. I pray that neither material possessions nor earthly accomplishments would have the slightest hold on her heart. As her husband, help me to model what it means to find my own meaning and worth in my identity as your son (Galatians 3:26).

Father, I pray that if we do feel discontentment, it would be toward the lost not having heard the gospel. Give us the joyful burden of longing to see sinners and strangers adopted into your family. Our time in this life is short—too short to spend seeking earthly things that will quickly fade. Give both me and my bride ultimate, steadfast contentment in you. May you be the primary pursuit of her life and mine, and let our marriage be a ready tool in your able hands.

In Jesus' name, amen.

Use these pages to journal your thoughts, write your own prayer, or both.

Date ________________

Day 5

That She Would Be Filled with Peace

Humble yourselves, therefore, under the mighty hand of God so that at the proper time he may exalt you, casting all your anxieties on him, because he cares for you.

---

1 Peter 5:6–7

Father, you are in total control. The universe is in the palm of your hand, yet you still discern my thoughts from afar (Isaiah 40:12; Psalm 139:2). By your sovereignty, the world rotates on its axis and my very cells are held together. Thank you for being in control! I know I can find rest in your will and that I can trust your goodness no matter what life brings. I'm forever grateful that you're powerful so I don't have to be. You rule with justice, mercy, grace, and love; you alone deserve all glory.

Your Word says you give peace beyond understanding—a peace not of this world (John 14:27). I pray that you give my wife deep, lasting peace. Help her trust you and find rest in doing so. I ask that you still her heart from whatever may be troubling her. Life gets so hectic at times, and I know she sometimes carries undue pressure throughout her day. Release her of it. Help her to see you. Remind her that you're in control, you're sovereign, and above all, that you're her good, loving, and faithful God. I ask that you lighten whatever burdens she's feeling right now and replace them with your inexplicable peace (Philippians 4:7). Flood her heart with feelings of rest that can only come from you. Fill her with such life and joy that even she can't explain it except by looking to you. Rid her mind of all fear, anxiety, and worry.

I also pray that our household would be a place governed by the same peace Jesus described. Let our conversations overflow with patience for each other and confidence in your sovereignty. You are King over all, including our home. Fill us with your Holy Spirit in increasing measure, and multiply our peace by your grace.

In Jesus' name, amen.

Use these pages to journal your thoughts, write your own prayer, or both.

Date ________________

Day 6
For Her Physical Health

Beloved, I pray that all may go well with you and that you may be in good health, as it goes well with your soul.

---

3 John 2

Each day is a new blessing from you. And I realize that our health is a gift, not a guarantee. Lord, thank you for the days you've given me and every ounce of health I've experienced. You know the ins and outs of my physiology—you formed me in my mother's womb (Psalm 139:13; Jeremiah 1:5) and you know, in detail, every single hair on my head (Matthew 10:30). There is nothing about my health or my bride's that is a mystery to you, and I rest in knowing that you are sovereign, no matter what we face.

Father, I pray for my wife's physical health and strength. I ask that you would protect her body from disease and illness. Keep her healthy and strong! Give her a unique appreciation for the energy she has, and make her aware of unique ways she can use it for your glory.

Even more than her physical health, I pray that "it goes well with [her] soul." You said in your Word that "bodily training is of some value," but "godliness is of value in every way, as it holds promise for the present life and also for the life to come" (1 Timothy 4:8). Help her remember the truth that her godliness is of eternal value! As her husband, I know I need to encourage her in her walk with you. Prompt me in ways to help her grow in her relationship with you. Be my leader as I learn each day what it means to lead and love her well.

In all things and in every way, you are sovereign. May you grant us both the maturity of faith to call on you as children during every instance of need—physical, spiritual, and otherwise—trusting in your goodness and faithfulness. Our flesh may fail, but God, you are the strength of our hearts, and our portion forever (Psalm 73:26).

In Jesus' name, amen.

Use these pages to journal your thoughts, write your own prayer, or both.

Date ________________

Day 7
Rest and Reflect

Then, because so many people were coming and going that they did not even have a chance to eat, he said to them, "Come with me by yourselves to a quiet place and get some rest."

Mark 6:31 NIV

Take time today to rest in who God is. Be still. Reflect on the prayers you've said and written over the past week. Use the space below to record how God has been working in your life and marriage.

Day 8
For Her Words

Let the words of my mouth and the meditation of my heart be acceptable in your sight, O Lord, my rock and my redeemer.

Psalm 19:14

Lord, by your word you called everything into existence. You simply spoke, and it was. Then you called it good! I'm in awe of your power and creative might, and I'm thankful for what you made. Thank you for crafting my wife just the way you did. You've made her beautiful inside and out, and you've given her a mind and heart after you. She is a treasure and a gift, and I'm forever grateful!

Father, I pray that you impress upon my wife the importance of her words and thoughts. Help her speak wisely and with discernment, not foolishly or flippantly. Holy Spirit, show her times when her words aren't honoring to you or useful for building others up. Give her the gift of self-control when she's tempted to gossip, and lovingly convict her heart. May the words of her mouth and the meditations of her heart be pleasing to you (Psalm 19:14).

Use her to encourage others and bring joy. Give her opportunities not only to speak life, but to share the gospel. Then, I pray that what she says bears fruit—in her life, my life, and the lives of everyone she meets.

Just as you willed my wife into being, you've graciously allowed me to be her husband. Thank you! She is one of your most obvious blessings in my life. Forgive me for the times when I've not spoken to her lovingly. Help me to also use my words wisely—to love her intentionally and build her up in ways that honor and glorify you (1 Thessalonians 5:11). Empower me to lead by example in how I speak to her, and show me areas where I can improve.

In Jesus' name, amen.

Use these pages to journal your thoughts, write your own prayer, or both.

Date ______________

Day 9

For Our Physical Intimacy

I adjure you, O daughters of Jerusalem, if you find my beloved, that you tell him I am sick with love.

Song of Solomon 5:8

Father, you are a relational God. You designed me to know and be known by you. Thank you for creating me in your image, with the capacity to experience and desire you daily. You are the ultimate prize—the only worthy pursuit in life! You're the only source of true satisfaction and complete joy.

While you have created me to ultimately glorify and worship you, you have also given me the desire and need for human relationship here on earth. When you created Adam, you said it was not good for him to be alone, so you gave him Eve (Genesis 2:18). In the same way, you've given me my wife; thank you for her!

I ask that you help us experience deeper physical intimacy in our marriage. Help my wife (and me) see and value sex the way you do. While I know I have a role to play in building her trust and vulnerability, I pray that you begin a work in her heart that gives her a deeper sense of its importance in our marriage. I pray that she would desire me and that I would desire her—that we would be "sick with love" for one another, as Solomon wrote. Then, I pray that when we're intimate it would glorify you and strengthen our bond as husband and wife.

God, let our physical intimacy be an indication of our emotional closeness and lifelong covenant with each other. Help us to serve each other's physical needs with purity, selflessness, and love. Thank you for the gift of sex. It is good, just as you created it to be! Grow us in this area, and help us to love each other with pure intentions and total transparency.

In Jesus' name, amen.

Use these pages to journal your thoughts, write your own prayer, or both.

Date ________________

Day 10

For Unshakable Gratitude

Therefore let us be grateful for receiving a
kingdom that cannot be shaken, and thus
let us offer to God acceptable worship, with
reverence and awe, for our God is a consuming
fire.

Hebrews 12:28–29

Father, your kingdom cannot be shaken! You reign over all with certainty, goodness, and complete sovereignty. There is no other god besides you; you alone are worthy of all glory, honor, and praise (Isaiah 45:5). May your will be done on earth and in heaven.

Let your will be done in my life as a man and as a husband. Show me areas where I need to repent and turn to you—areas where I've tried to control and seek identity in anything or anyone other than you. Root my heart and identity in the grace of your gospel; help me believe with every aspect of my being.

Thank you for my amazing wife! I ask that you flood her heart with the truth of who you are and what you've done in Christ. Remind her that she has received your unshakable kingdom, and let it overflow into rich, authentic gratitude in her life. From there, move her heart to worship you out of complete awe (Psalm 33:8).

Your Word says you are a consuming fire; let her be consumed by you. Overwhelm her heart with your greatness and goodness in such a way that puts everything else—even the smallest tasks and annoyances—into divine perspective. From there, give her sweet rest . . . the kind that only comes from being lost in you.

Thank you for our marriage and that we can walk alongside one another with you as our ultimate destination. Give us unity where it matters most, and help us love each other well in the day-to-day grind. You are the almighty King; you always have been, and you always will be.

In Jesus' name, amen.

Use these pages to journal your thoughts, write your own prayer, or both. **Date** ______________

Day 11

For Grace in Her Work

Let the favor of the Lord our God be upon us,
and establish the work of our hands upon us;
yes, establish the work of our hands!

Psalm 90:17

God, the work of your hands is perfect and complete. You reign over every atom and star, and you surely hold them together by the work of your hand. Thank you, Father, for the gift of work. By my vocation I am able to provide for my family's needs and add value to my community. Not only that, but you have commissioned me to participate in your work of saving your people through planting and watering seeds of the gospel (1 Corinthians 3:7). Establish the work of your hands through the work of mine. Use me however you will!

I also thank you for my wife's ability and capacity to work. Whether she's in our home or at her job, she goes forth only because you allow it. I pray that you would bless the work of her hands today. When she feels tired, energize her. When she feels worn-out, refresh her soul. If she's stressed, remind her of your sovereignty and give her peace.

I pray that she is a light to everyone she meets (Matthew 5:14). Give her inexplicable joy that is noticeable to unbelievers, and prompt her by your Holy Spirit to share your love with them at every opportunity. I thank you for her mind and her giftings; make her fruitful in whatever work she puts her hands to today (Ecclesiastes 9:10).

God, while I'm thankful for the ability to work in my vocation and earn a living, I'm more thankful that I don't have to work to earn my salvation—that my sins are forgiven forever in Christ. Thank you for your inexhaustible grace! You truly are a loving, forgiving, and exceedingly good God. Remind my wife of her eternal security in you—that she is saved by grace alone, through faith alone, in Christ alone.

In Jesus' name, amen.

Use these pages to journal your thoughts, write your own prayer, or both.

Date ____________________

Day 12

For Emotional Safety and Vulnerability

For God gave us a spirit not of fear but of power and love and self-control.

---

2 Timothy 1:7

God, you are the Great Designer. Every facet of creation emanates your glory! From the farthest star to the smallest neuron firing in my mind, you've designed every particle masterfully. Of all your creation, I can only perceive and appreciate a small portion—and what I do manage to grasp, I grasp inadequately. Father, I rest in your sovereignty and find great comfort in your constant care over all you have made—including my beautiful bride (Psalm 104).

You have designed my wife very well—intricately and with great complexity. Help me to appreciate every facet of the woman you've given me, and grant me discernment on how to better encourage her. God, if I'm honest, sometimes one of the hardest parts of my wife to understand is her emotions. We're just wired differently. Yet, I know you've created her exactly has you have with your divine purposes in mind. Please give me an extraordinary understanding and perception of her emotions, and graciously use me to contribute to her emotional health.

Father, help my wife feel safe being emotionally vulnerable with me, and help her understand everything she feels within the context of how and why you've created her. I pray that you'd give her a supernatural sense of what thoughts and feelings are from you and which ones are attacks meant to cause harm (1 Peter 5:8–9).

I cherish the times when we connect on deep emotional levels; help me lead us there often. Guide our conversations and allow our friendship to flourish. Thank you for this amazing woman you've given me. Cover her heart and mind, protect her, and help me to do the same as far as I am able.

In Jesus' name, amen.

Use these pages to journal your thoughts, write your own prayer, or both.

Date ______________

Day 13

For a Vibrant Prayer Life

And this is the confidence that we have toward him, that if we ask anything according to his will he hears us.

---

1 John 5:14

Father, what a gift it is to be able to talk to you. Through your son, Jesus, you have torn the veil and given us access to your throne of grace (Hebrews 4:16). Thank you! Help me to never lose sight of the wonder and privilege it is to pray. And thank you that it's not a one-way conversation. You have spoken clearly through your Word, and you minister to me through the power of your Holy Spirit. Only a loving and good God would do what you have done.

God, I pray that you enliven my wife's prayer life. Deepen her reliance on you, and compel her to bring her every dream, concern, worry, fear, and victory to you in prayer. Help her understand what it means to approach you with confidence in Christ—knowing that she is made righteous and holy because of his sacrifice.

I pray that you burden her heart for people who need prayer. Help her see opportunities to pray with and for others throughout her day. Solidify your Word in her heart, and remind her of what you've said whenever she approaches you. I pray that her prayers would be powerful and faith filled—Spirit-led and full of righteous confidence.

Finally, help me lead our family well in this area. Continue to teach me what it means to pray; impress upon my heart its importance. Don't let me grow lazy in my prayer life, and forgive me for times when I've not taken it seriously. I know your grace abounds, but I also know that I need as much face-to-face time with you as possible. Hear our prayers, God. Answer each one according to your will, and build our faith every step of the way.

In Jesus' name, amen.

Use these pages to journal your thoughts, write your own prayer, or both.

Date ____________

Day 14
Rest and Reflect

You keep him in perfect peace whose mind is stayed on you, because he trusts in you.

Isaiah 26:3

Take time today to rest in who God is. Be still. Reflect on the prayers you've said and written over the past week. Use the space below to record how God has been working in your life and marriage.

Day 15
Guard Her Heart

Keep your heart with all vigilance, for from it flow the springs of life.

Proverbs 4:23

Dear God, you are the author and perfecter of our faith (Hebrews 12:2). You've called us into relationship with you, and you are faithful to complete the work you began in our hearts. You finish everything you start with skill and precision! Thank you for drawing us near, opening our ears to hear, and making us sensitive to your voice. And thank you for never giving up on us through the process.

Father, I thank you for the work you're doing in my wife. Please continue it! I'm in awe of your Spirit in her and humbled that I get to watch what you're doing. Please help her guard her heart with vigilance. I pray that she can quickly identify thoughts, intentions, and actions that may hurt her heart or cause her to stray from faith. Protect her mind from fear, anxiety, and anything else that steals her focus from you.

Also, guard her heart from attacks of the enemy; make her aware of them and help her stand on your Word as she fights against them (Ephesians 6:11–17). I pray that you'd lovingly convict her of any areas of sin or idolatry—any area where she's elevating things, circumstances, or people to places of authority in her life where they shouldn't be. Remind her that you're her ultimate source of joy, security, identity, and strength.

God, help me help my wife. As her husband, I want your absolute best for her. Give me the right words to say and wisdom to say them at the best time (Proverbs 15:23). Most of all, thank you for your faithful hand working in both of our lives and our marriage. We'd be lost without you, but with you, we are found, loved, and secure.

In Jesus' name, amen.

Use these pages to journal your thoughts, write your own prayer, or both.

Date ______________

Day 16
For Newness of Life

I have been crucified with Christ. It is no longer I who live, but Christ who lives in me. And the life I now live in the flesh I live by faith in the Son of God, who loved me and gave himself for me.

Galatians 2:20

Father, the truth of your Word never fails and never fades. It never grows old or stale, and you never change (James 1:17)! From everlasting to everlasting, you are God (Psalm 90:2). Thank you for giving me new life in Jesus. Help me understand what it means to die to myself—to be crucified with Christ—and to be made alive in you. Help me live as a new creation (2 Corinthians 5:17).

I pray that you give my wife an unmistakable sense of her new life in Christ. I know she's hard on herself; she often focuses on the mistakes she makes and the doubts she has. Help her see that you're working in her, sanctifying her, and refining her every day. Help her realize that it's not her perfection that makes her loved, but your perfection (Galatians 2:21).

She knows that she has new life intellectually—in her mind—but help her know it and believe it on even deeper levels. May the reality of her new life in Christ penetrate her heart, all the way to the core of her being. From there, I pray that she'd walk in complete freedom, with abundant joy, hope, and peace that comes from you. Make her every step secure, regardless of the terrain or circumstance.

God, my wife is a gift and a treasure. Thank you that I get to be her husband! Thank you that you put us together to walk this journey of sanctification. Thank you for the life we get to share. Teach me to love her well and lead our family with wisdom. You are Lord of our household; may we glorify you in all we do.

In Jesus' name, amen.

Use these pages to journal your thoughts, write your own prayer, or both.

Date ____________

Day 17
For Freedom to Forgive

And whenever you stand praying, forgive, if you have anything against anyone, so that your Father also who is in heaven may forgive you your trespasses.

Mark 11:25

Father, your Word says that you've removed our transgressions from us as far as the east is from the west (Psalm 103:12). In Christ, we no longer need to earn our righteousness, but are made righteous by his blood. Thank you for your endless, boundless forgiveness! Thank you that there is nothing that can separate me from your love when I place my trust in you (Romans 8:38–39).

I ask that my wife experiences the freedom that comes from being generously forgiven in Christ. I pray that she learns to forgive others as she has been forgiven. If she's holding grudges or harboring bitterness, I pray that she would be reminded of your reckless grace and your call to give it to others. Not only that, but I pray that she would give grace wholeheartedly, without reservation, to those who have wronged her.

God, I know sin brings earthly consequences—that some relationships may never be the same, even after the sin is forgiven—but I pray that my wife remains free of bitterness and unforgiveness in her heart, regardless of consequences.

Also, I pray that our marriage would be a place of generous forgiveness and ongoing reconciliation. We're both sinners saved by grace, so there will be times when we sin against each other. Help her forgive me when I need it, and help me to forgive her whenever she needs it. You have not held our sin against us; I pray that whatever issues we face, we reconcile and not hold sin against each other. May your grace reign in our lives and in our marriage.

In Jesus' name, amen.

Use these pages to journal your thoughts, write your own prayer, or both.

Date ______________

Day 18
For Compassion and Empathy

Put on then, as God's chosen ones, holy and beloved, compassionate hearts, kindness, humility, meekness, and patience.

Colossians 3:12

God, your mercies are new every morning (Lamentations 3:22–23). Not a single day passes where your grace fails to flood the earth. You hold everything in your hand, and you promise to care for creation down to the smallest detail. There is no end to your compassion, care, and grace! Help me understand, just a little more, the depth of your compassion. Help me show it to others, starting with my wife. Show me opportunities when I can care for her and model your compassion in our home. Forgive me for times when I've been harsh, and help me repair any trust I've broken.

Father, also help my wife reflect your compassionate character. Give her a profound understanding of your compassionate love for her, and let it pour out of her through her words and actions. She is created in your image; may she reflect your mercy richly today. If ever she forgets, Lord, remind her! Fill her with your Holy Spirit, and use her to be a light to everyone she meets. Let her abound with every good work as she places her trust and identity in you, not to earn your love, but because of it!

God, you have called us to love our neighbors as ourselves (Matthew 22:34–40). That one truth is the root of all compassion. Spur our hearts to show kindness to people in our lives who need it. Open our eyes to see opportunities; don't let us be distracted by meaningless things. Use us and use our marriage to reflect your kindness, mercy, and compassion. God, we are yours. Unify us in our purpose and strengthen our marriage—all for your glory!

In Jesus' name, amen.

Use these pages to journal your thoughts, write your own prayer, or both.

Date ________________

Day 19

Give Her Confidence in Our Covenant

But from the beginning of creation, "God made them male and female." "Therefore a man shall leave his father and mother and hold fast to his wife, and the two shall become one flesh." So they are no longer two but one flesh. What therefore God has joined together, let not man separate.

Mark 10:6–9

God, please make our marriage stronger. You have proven time and time again that you are a God of your word and that covenant is important to you. Thank you for your untiring faithfulness and pursuit of your people, despite their—our—unfaithfulness to you. You alone love with perfect patience. There is none like you!

Just as your covenants with your people matter to you, I know our marriage covenant is important in your eyes. Bind us closer together every day. Unify us and help us to walk as one flesh.

I ask that you give my wife confidence in our marriage because of you. Help her see and value our covenant as you do. If ever she grows weary, remind her that you are her strength through everything (Isaiah 40:30–31). If ever she wavers in her commitment, renew her faith. I know I'm not perfect, and I have sinned against her many times. I know that at times she may feel like our marriage is hard. Help us to walk together as one through anything!

Lord, help us not to doubt the work you're doing in our hearts through our marriage. Thank you for knowing us intimately—our faults and all—and still choosing to love us! Help us to love each other in the same way. Help us to live transparently and with integrity. Give us the ability to be honest with each other even when it's hardest; then give us the supernatural ability to love despite our imperfections.

Help me lead in this area. Holy Spirit, guide us today. What therefore you have joined together, let man not separate!

In Jesus' name, amen.

Use these pages to journal your thoughts, write your own prayer, or both.

Date ______________

Day 20
For Quality Friendships

Two are better than one, because they have a good reward for their toil. For if they fall, one will lift up his fellow. But woe to him who is alone when he falls and has not another to lift him up!

Ecclesiastes 4:9–10

God, you are the author of life and the lover of our souls (Acts 3:14–15). You have created us for relationship—with you first, but also with others. Thank you for making me in your image and giving me enriching friendships—both with other men but also with my wife. She is my best friend and your most obvious blessing in my life. Thank you for the gift of a wife who is also a friend.

Lord, please help my wife's friend life. Two are truly better than one. I pray that you help deepen her current relationships while also leading her into new friendships with other women. Where there is an unhealthy friendship, I ask that you'd make her aware of it and give her confidence to pursue health, whatever that means. God, I also ask that you'd give her friends that will speak into her life and uplift her. Bring older, wiser women to her that will encourage her in her walk with you and provide her wisdom in the decisions she makes (Proverbs 15:22). I pray that she would build strong, godly friendships that can withstand even the hardest times.

Lastly, I pray that the time she invests in others will prove fruitful. Use my wife to help other women in their understanding of your Word and application of what it says. Use her testimony to encourage and use her words to build up. I pray that you'd make her an unfailing light to those she befriends and a beacon of hope to everyone she meets.

As her husband, help me model what it means to build quality, Christ-centered friendships. Convict me in ways that I can grow and lead her in this area. Thank you for my beautiful wife—my helper and my friend (Genesis 2:18). May our friendships with each other and with others be glorifying to you in every way.

In Jesus' name, amen.

Use these pages to journal your thoughts, write your own prayer, or both.

Date ________________

Day 21
Rest and Reflect

In peace I will both lie down and sleep; for you alone, O Lord, make me dwell in safety.

Psalm 4:8

Take time today to rest in who God is. Be still. Reflect on the prayers you've said and written over the past week. Use the space below to record how God has been working in your life and marriage.

Day 22

As She Runs Her Race

Do you not know that in a race all the runners run, but only one receives the prize? So run that you may obtain it. Every athlete exercises self-control in all things. They do it to receive a perishable wreath, but we an imperishable. So I do not run aimlessly; I do not box as one beating the air.

---

1 Corinthians 9:24–26

God, you are worthy of every moment and every breath I have to give. You alone are worthy of worship, and you alone prove faithful! I will spend my life in awe and wonder of who you are, with deep thankfulness for all you've done. May my words, actions, and attitudes be glorifying to you, and may the motivations of my heart make you glad (Psalm 19:14). I know I'm not perfect, which is why I'm forever grateful for your grace! Refine me and make me holy, for my good and your glory.

Thank you for my amazing wife. Thank you for putting her in my life and using her to make me a better man. Lord, I pray that you'd fill her with faith today. Help her to understand fully the race she is running. I realize that it's easy for her to lose perspective—just like it's easy for me—and that the daily grind of life can make her weary. I pray that you'd reinvigorate her and enliven her faith. Remind her that she is your daughter and a citizen of your everlasting kingdom (Philippians 3:20). Let her ultimate prize be you, Jesus! Give her self-control in all things, and let her every action and word be well aimed. Stir her affections for you, and refresh her appreciation of your grace and goodness.

God, as my wife runs the race you have for her, make her feet swift and her heart strong. Open her eyes to how powerful you are! Give her faith to ask big things of you. Give her faith to speak boldly in love. And give her faith to say no to good things because she is pursuing your absolute best.

I love her with all my heart, God. Help me to build her up with words of encouragement and faith. Help me lead her well as I remember for myself the race I am in and that you, too, are my ultimate prize.

In Jesus' name, amen.

Use these pages to journal your thoughts, write your own prayer, or both.

Date ______________

Day 23
That She Would Walk in Patience

I therefore, a prisoner for the Lord, urge you to walk in a manner worthy of the calling to which you have been called, with all humility and gentleness, with patience, bearing with one another in love.

Ephesians 4:1–2

Holy Spirit, thank you for your presence, your counsel, and your love. It is only by you and through you that eternal and holy fruit is produced in my life as well as my wife's.

As I read your Word, you are so faithful to teach me about the process of growth and production. Growth requires a divine presence and power outside of ourselves. Only you can cause and create growth (1 Corinthians 3:6). You allow me to take part in the planting and watering processes, but the growth comes from you. Root my mind in this knowledge and understanding.

Humbly I come and ask that you would produce patience within my wife's heart and mine. Praying for patience (for me and for my wife) is not an easy or desirable request, but nonetheless I ask you for it.

While the apostle Paul was in prison, he wrote to the Ephesians, urging them to walk in a manner worthy of the calling they had received. I humbly echo Paul's urging for my wife. Help her to walk in her calling—to walk in patience, humility, and gentleness. Please continue to show her how to bear with others (and me) in love.

God, you know the importance of the production of patience in our lives, and you cause its growth—thank you! Not only does this fruit help my wife and me endure trials of many kinds, but it also helps unify us as the body of Christ (James 1:2–4). To you, God, be all the glory.

In Jesus' name, amen.

Use these pages to journal your thoughts, write your own prayer, or both.

Date ________________

Day 24

That She Would Be Anchored in Christ

We have this hope as an anchor for the soul, firm and secure.

Hebrews 6:19 CSB

Father, you alone are my rock (Psalm 18:31). You alone.

As I look back through all I've experienced and the trials I've endured, you have never failed me. You are forever faithful! Thank you for your undying love and faithfulness. And, as I look forward, I find comfort knowing that you are in control—you are sovereign over all (Colossians 1:17).

God, help my bride feel a sense of peace and joy in knowing that you are her rock and refuge. Anchor her soul in you, Jesus. Make her hope firm and secure as she goes about her day today. Fill her with your Holy Spirit as she interacts with others, and let her words reflect her eternal security in you.

Help me to be a constant reminder to her. If she ever forgets, help me to consistently lead her back to the gospel and remind her of her worth and value as one created in your image, God (Genesis 1:27).

Jesus, thank you for being the anchor of our salvation! Thank you for saving us from ourselves and for continually molding both my wife and me into your image. Continue your good work in and through us today. May our marriage reflect your love for your church, and may our ministry to each other be pleasing and glorifying to you.

Let your hope be the anthem of our lives. Help us both to never forget that you are our anchor forever, firm and secure, steadfast, and never failing.

In Jesus' name, amen.

Use these pages to journal your thoughts, write your own prayer, or both.

Date ______________

Day 25

That She Would Forget What Is Behind

Brothers and sisters, I do not consider myself to have attained this. Instead I am single-minded: forgetting the things that are behind and reaching out for the things that are ahead.

Philippians 3:13 NET

Lord, as I look back, I am amazed at all you've done in my life. You've given me incalculable graces and mercies; there is truly none like you! You called me by name, softened my heart, granted me salvation, and you continue to make me a better man each day—one who can somehow glorify you (and even that is only by your grace!). God, help me to never forget your goodness as the Israelites did (Psalm 106:21), but help me to forget what's behind as Paul teaches, that I may reach out more intently for all you are.

God, I pray the same for my wife. May she never forget all you have done for her and for us. You have brought us so far and through so much—pain, hardship, struggles, and frustrations. Let us never forget your goodness! On the other hand, may we, as a couple, quickly forget all the things that are behind and reach out for all that is ahead.

As I look at my wife and the person she is today, I see the incredible, beautiful woman you gave me. I see a woman who is being molded and transformed every day. I see your daughter whom you are calling unto yourself with every waking moment—calling her out of darkness and further into your light (1 Peter 2:9). Help her to never look back to former things, but instead show her how to keep her eyes on you. I pray that she would see her regrets and mistakes as mere mileposts on her grander journey toward you. Let her every loss, mistake, regret, and misstep pale in comparison to your surpassing worth and goodness (Philippians 3:8).

Make us both single-minded in our love for and pursuit of you, forgetting the things that are behind and reaching out for the things that are ahead.

In Jesus' name, amen.

Use these pages to journal your thoughts, write your own prayer, or both.

Date ________________

Day 26

For Protection of Her Thought Life

We destroy arguments and every lofty opinion raised against the knowledge of God, and take every thought captive to obey Christ.

---

2 Corinthians 10:5

God, as the heavens are higher than the earth, so are your ways and thoughts higher than mine (Isaiah 55:9). You have made foolish the wisdom of this world (1 Corinthians 1:20)! I'm more thankful than ever to rest in the hands of a good, wise, and loving God. Remembering your power and sovereignty fills me with peaceful wonder. I'm forever grateful that your foolishness is wiser than my greatest wisdom and your weakness is stronger than my mightiest feat (1 Corinthians 1:25).

I pray for my wife's thought life—help her to take every thought captive and make it obedient to Christ. As she goes about her day today, Holy Spirit, minister to her. Remind her that she is your daughter, hand-selected by you to be your daughter. Give her an unshakable confidence in her identity because of Jesus—that she is bought and paid for by the blood, accepted without qualification, and delighted in by you, the God of all creation. Protect her mind from attacks of the enemy.

I pray that any discouragement, lies, insecurities, and fears would fall dead at the foot of the cross, and that she would experience supernatural freedom in her thought life like nothing she's felt ever before.

God, thank you for hearts and minds that are free from slavery because of you. Help us both to take stray thoughts, arguments, and lofty opinions captive and make them obedient to you. Give us unity in that, and grant us discernment to help one another whenever we can. Thank you for your enduring, sanctifying work in our lives. Continue to conform us to your image (Romans 8:29).

In Jesus' name, amen.

Use these pages to journal your thoughts, write your own prayer, or both.

Date ____________________

Day 27
For Purpose, Perspective, and Patience

Not only that, but we rejoice in our sufferings, knowing that suffering produces endurance, and endurance produces character, and character produces hope, and hope does not put us to shame, because God's love has been poured into our hearts through the Holy Spirit who has been given to us.

Romans 5:3–5

God, thank you for your divine plan. In you we have context for our very existence; we can have purpose in this life: to glorify you and to experience your grace! Knowing that you have a purpose for me—for us—gives me perspective during trials and patience to endure. In you we have hope both in this life and the next (1 Corinthians 15:19)!

Father, I ask that you give my wife a deep sense of your everlasting purpose in her life. Help her see your hand at work in her and through her. Let your hope fuel her thoughts, actions, and desires. You said that we'd experience trials of many kinds in this life. Help her to remember you and your promises through each one. Help her rejoice in you during hard times, knowing that it builds patience, character, and hope.

You promised that hope in you would never put us to shame (Romans 5:5). Remind my wife of that today. Remind her of the hope she has in you whenever she grows impatient, worries, or feels weak. Help her to rest in you whenever she's frustrated, and guide me in ways that I can help her most.

Help me remember to rejoice during trials as well. Teach me to lead her in putting our hope in you, no matter what is going on in life and no matter how we're feeling. You are the Alpha and the Omega—the beginning and the end—and you're the same yesterday, today, and forever (Hebrews 13:8). Thank you that in you, we have eternal hope!

In Jesus' name, amen.

Use these pages to journal your thoughts, write your own prayer, or both.

Date ________________

Day 28
Rest and Reflect

And he said,
"My presence will go with you,
and I will give you rest."

Exodus 33:14

Take time today to rest in who God is. Be still. Reflect on the prayers you've said and written over the past week. Use the space below to record how God has been working in your life and marriage.

Day 29
For Otherworldly Peace

"Peace I leave with you; my peace I give to you. Not as the world gives do I give to you. Let not your hearts be troubled, neither let them be afraid."

John 14:27

Lord, there are times when mental battles rage and finding lasting peace seems like a pipe dream. This world is marred by sin, chaotic and tumultuous, prone to disorder. In my sin nature, I often let that chaos and tumult invade my thoughts. I forget how trustworthy you are, how caring you are, and how much you have already done to prove your faithfulness in my life. Lord, in those times when I'm anxious (and even now), help my unbelief (Mark 9:24). Call out and calm the storms in my mind, flooding my heart with inexplicable calm.

God, just as I've struggled finding peace, I know my wife often struggles as well. Free her from worry and anxiety. Comfort her when she feels overrun with anxious thoughts. She can't control what people say, think, or do; help her remember that truth and take refuge in you (Psalm 118:8). She can't control what happens around her; remind her that you are alive and working in all things for her good. Enliven her faith by the power of your Word—be her anchor, firm and secure (Hebrews 6:19 NIV).

God, this is an area where I desperately need your help: empathy. So often, I fail to empathize with my wife when she needs it most. I lose patience. Too many times, my first reaction to her anxiousness is to minimize it and even dismiss it. When I do either, I'm not loving her well or helping in any way. Make me aware of times when I can support her, pray for her, listen to her, and encourage her with your promises.

Thank you for the wife you have given me. I love her with all my heart and want your absolute best for her. Help me to lead and love her well by being an empathetic peacemaker and encourager in our household.

In Jesus' name, amen.

Use these pages to journal your thoughts, write your own prayer, or both.

Date ________________

Day 30
Clothe Her with Strength and Dignity

Strength and dignity are her clothing, and she laughs at the time to come.

Proverbs 31:25

There is none like you, Lord! Your power is unmatched and your ways are perfect. "You rule over all the kingdoms of the nations. In your hand are power and might, so that none is able to withstand you" (2 Chronicles 20:6). Truly, you alone are worthy of worship. What gets me the most is that you, the God of the universe, have found fit to love me and give yourself up for me. Thank you for loving me enough to save me! Because of you, I'll never be the same. Knowing and being known by you has turned my world upside down for the better.

I pray that you'd give my wife a vivid sense of her identity as your daughter—one you loved enough to call by name and save by grace. Clothe her with strength and dignity that is unmistakably visible on her face. I pray that she'd feel spiritually strong, able to fight off and take captive thoughts that aren't of you. I pray that she'd feel mentally and emotionally fortified—able to focus her thoughts on all that is true, noble, right, pure, lovely, and admirable (Philippians 4:8 NIV). Finally, I pray that she'd feel dignified—worthy of respect and honor. Give her a lighthearted, carefree freedom that only comes from knowing and being known by you.

I love my wife: her mind, her personality, everything about her. When I look at her, I see a beautiful woman inside and out. Thank you for the woman you've given me! She is truly a person of strength and dignity. God, I pray that you'd teach me to love her selflessly, with every ounce of honor and respect she deserves. Let your transformational grace and love that I've experienced translate into how I love my wife. I consider it a massive honor to be her husband. Thank you for entrusting her heart to my care.

In Jesus' name, amen.

Use these pages to journal your thoughts, write your own prayer, or both.

Date ________________

Day 31
Give Her the Heart of a Peacemaker

Blessed are the peacemakers, for they shall be called sons of God.

Matthew 5:9

God, you are the ultimate peacemaker. You pierced the darkness with light, you calmed the storm, and you set the captives free—all in the name of peacemaking. You humbled yourself to death on a cross in order to reconcile your people back to you. You satisfied the requirements of the law because we couldn't, and you bore the weight of our sin so we wouldn't. Be praised! You truly deserve all honor and glory forever!

Lord, it's so easy to let internal frustrations and fears create discord in external relationships. This is the opposite of how you've called me to live. Forgive me for the times when I haven't actively made peace in our household. Help me identify opportunities to emulate your peacemaking character, particularly in my relationship with my wife.

I also pray that you'd give my wife a heart of a peacemaker. Instill in her a desire to see wrongs made right, and to bring justice where it's missing. Help her to make sense of chaotic situations and to see a clear path toward peace where there seems to be none. Whether she's with friends, at work, or taking care of our children, allow her the awareness and fortitude to defuse frustrating situations quickly and equitably.

We both desperately need your help in this area. Give us wisdom to discern the difference between peace*keeping* and peace*making*. Peacekeepers avoid conflict of all kinds at all costs, whereas peacemakers acknowledge that hard conversations are sometimes necessary for true peace and reconciliation. Grant us the words to say and the means to say them in your perfect timing and with motivations that are pure. Holy Spirit, reign in my wife's heart with your everlasting peace and allow it to overflow into every facet of her life.

In Jesus' name, amen.

Use these pages to journal your thoughts, write your own prayer, or both. **Date ________________**

Day 32
For Watchful Diligence

She watches over the affairs of her household
and does not eat the bread of idleness.

Proverbs 31:27 NIV

Father, as I marvel at your creation, I'm filled with gratitude. Every plant, flower, beast, and insect diligently lives, eats, grows, and multiplies, all by your flawless design. You hold the universe together, atom by atom, cell by cell (Colossians 1:17). From the smallest particle to the largest galaxy, your diligent, loving care is evident everywhere. Your Word says you created us in your image—parts of you have been passed on to us, including our ability and desire to take diligent care of all you've entrusted to our hands. God, help me steward all you've given me in a way that honors you and reflects your character—starting with my wife.

Thank you for my wife's diligence in caring for our household. Thank you for how she loves me. She's not perfect, and neither am I, so please let your grace flood our home as we learn to love each other well and communicate through every struggle. I pray that you'd give her a watchful vigilance in caring for all "the affairs of her household." Inspire her to think creatively as she solves problems and creates solutions. I pray that she'd find eternal purpose in even the most mundane tasks—whether she's paying bills, watering plants, working in her vocation, or planning a family event. It's not all up to her (I know we're called to work together), but I pray that whatever tasks or burdens fall into her purview, she would find joy and gladness in diligently caring for them.

You have blessed us in innumerable ways, O God! I can't possibly number them all, let alone do anything to deserve your goodness. I pray that my wife would be filled with gratitude and joy for all you've given us, and as a result, care diligently with watchfulness over everything you've entrusted to us.

In Jesus' name, amen.

Use these pages to journal your thoughts, write your own prayer, or both. **Date ______________**

Day 33
For a Wise Fear of the Lord

The fear of the LORD is the beginning of wisdom, and the knowledge of the Holy One is insight.

Proverbs 9:10

I'm so thankful that you are a gracious God, and that when you look at me, you see Jesus' perfection instead of my own sin (Romans 3:22). Without your imputed righteousness, I'd be without a hope in the world, but with it, I have every promise in the universe! Your free gift of grace makes no sense, yet I receive it by faith and with praise on my lips. I never want to forget how good and how holy you are. Nor do I want to lose sight of your vast, eternal scope and power. Father, I understand that I am but a man and you are the one true, mighty, holy, and powerful God. I gladly fear you, but I'm ever thankful that I need not be afraid.

Your Word says, "Charm is deceptive, and beauty is fleeting; but a woman who fears the Lord is to be praised" (Proverbs 31:30 NIV). Instill in my wife's heart a healthy understanding of what it means to fear you in the way that David meant in Proverbs.

Whatever she is doing right now, fill her with awe and wonder as she sees you for the God that you are. Give her a clear vision of your might and mercy, your grandeur and grace. By your Holy Spirit, well up inside her a desire to worship you as the only one who is worthy. And as a result, Father, I pray that she would have wisdom beyond her years. I pray that every decision my wife makes, every word she says, and every plan she creates would flourish because of her wisdom that comes from fearing you.

Help me to lead her in learning, understanding, and believing your Word. Help me lead our household in full light of your holiness and grace. "As for me and my house, we will serve the Lord" (Joshua 24:15). Grant me the grace I need to lead and love my wife well.

In Jesus' name, amen.

Use these pages to journal your thoughts, write your own prayer, or both.

Date ______________

Day 34
For Faith to Move Mountains

"For truly, I say to you, if you have faith like a grain of mustard seed, you will say to this mountain, 'Move from here to there,' and it will move, and nothing will be impossible for you."

Matthew 17:20

God, you have no limits. There is nothing you can't do! In you all things hold together, and by your voice you brought the universe into existence (Colossians 1:17). You are not bound by time and space, yet you entered humanity through your Son, to redeem and save your people. I am humbled by and thankful for your power and might!

Father, I ask that you give my wife unwavering faith that is rooted in knowledge of your character and intimate relationship with you. May she look at the mountains before her through eyes of faith and see you—our bigger, mightier God. Give her the gift of faith. Arrest her heart and captivate her sense of wonder; then give her courage to act with quick obedience, trusting in you as her strength, her conqueror, and her redeemer.

I also pray that she sees herself through those same eyes of faith. Let her confidence and self-worth be grounded and established in you. It's so easy for her to compare herself to other women and feel like she's unworthy, less-than, or lacking. Help her to see herself as you see her—righteous, justified, beautifully made, and worthy of love.

I pray that you make her a mighty woman of faith, like the woman Jesus spoke to when he said, "O woman, great is your faith! Be it done for you as you desire" (Matthew 15:28). Thank you for my bride, and thank you that I get to be her husband!

In Jesus' name, amen.

Use these pages to journal your thoughts, write your own prayer, or both.

Date ______________

Day 35
Rest and Reflect

The Lord is my shepherd; I shall not want. He makes me lie down in green pastures. He leads me beside still waters.
He restores my soul.

Psalm 23:1–3

Take time today to rest in who God is. Be still. Reflect on the prayers you've said and written over the past week. Use the space below to record how God has been working in your life and marriage.

Day 36

That She Would Be Fruitful

But the fruit of the Spirit is love, joy, peace, patience, kindness, goodness, faithfulness, gentleness, self-control; against such things there is no law.

Galatians 5:22–23

Nothing in this world compares to you, O Lord! "You have multiplied, O LORD my God, your wondrous deeds and your thoughts toward us; none can compare with you! I will proclaim and tell of them, yet they are more than can be told" (Psalm 40:5). Your ways are infinitely higher and better than my own (Isaiah 55:9). In your wisdom you have called me to live in ways that will always lead to my present flourishing and eternal good. In addition, you have given me a helper who continually transforms my heart and enables me to live a changed life. Lead me in bearing fruit, and help my wife to do the same.

God, may my wife bear fruit that is a pleasing aroma to you. Let the work of your Holy Spirit be evident in every facet of her life. As she loves, let her love with selflessness and freedom. Let her heart be filled with joy and peace, regardless of the circumstance she is facing. Grant her patience as she goes about her day; don't let her be bogged down by menial frustrations, but instead, give her an inexplicable ability to endure with grace and poise. Afford her abundant measures of kindness and goodness toward others, and help her actions spark conversations that make much of you while providing opportunities to share the gospel. And when she's alone, give her a faithful, self-controlled heart. Where she needs restraint, may she have it without question. Thank you for the gift of your Holy Spirit, and for helping us to live in ways that honor you.

Finally, thank you for the amazing wife you've given me; she is my best friend and favorite person. Help her to shine as a beacon of hope and light for you, and use me however you see fit to encourage her in that. Make her a clear and bright reflection of your goodness as she bears the fruits of your Spirit in abundance.

In Jesus' name, amen.

Use these pages to journal your thoughts, write your own prayer, or both.

Date ______________

Day 37
For Blessed Self-Forgetfulness

Let each of you look not only to his own interests, but also to the interests of others.

Philippians 2:4

God, you're good enough, big enough, and worthy enough to warrant all my praise! Who else is like you? Who is a rock but you? Who else holds the universe in their hand? None but you! Even knowing that truth, it's so easy to lose focus on you and become focused on myself. Our culture is obsessed with self-actualization, and if I'm honest, in my flesh I am too. You are enough, Jesus. Oh, that I would truly believe that with every fiber of my being! You are all I need for purpose and joy in this life; let every other pursuit fall to the wayside if ever they compete for my affection.

Father, I echo that same plea for my wife. Be her *enough* (2 Corinthians 9:8). Let her every deep desire and longing be fulfilled in you and you alone. So much so that she'd be blessed with true self-forgetfulness. Neither of us could ever muster authentic humility or self-forgetfulness aside from your help. Fix her gaze (and mine) upon you and remind her heart of who you are: the One "who forms the mountains, creates the wind, and reveals his thoughts to man, the one who makes the dawn out of darkness and strides on the heights of the earth" (Amos 4:13 CSB). So preoccupy our minds with you that even the most tumultuous circumstance poses no threat. Consume us with your fire and move in power in our lives.

Lord, as we forget ourselves, may we learn to serve one another with pure motives. Mark our home with genuine love that is others-focused, instead of being filled with selfish desire. Fortify our marriage by your Word, and be the center of our family. Unify us in all things that matter most to you. I thank you for the life I get to build with my beautiful bride. Bless us with the sweet gift of self-forgetfulness!

In Jesus' name, amen.

Use these pages to journal your thoughts, write your own prayer, or both. **Date _______________**

Day 38
Help Her Hunger and Thirst for Righteousness

Blessed are those who hunger and thirst for righteousness, for they shall be satisfied.

Matthew 5:6

David prayed, "I delight to do your will, O my God; your law is within my heart" (Psalm 40:8). He also asked that the words of his mouth and the meditations of his heart would be pleasing to you. Lord, let those be our prayers as well! The good news of the gospel is that we are given salvation from sin, but it doesn't end there! The gospel also means that we are no longer slaves to sin and death. Day by day, we are being molded and refined into the likeness of your Son, Jesus. Thank you for the sanctifying power of your gospel in our lives! God, make my wife and me hungry and thirsty for righteousness. I pray that sin would not agree with us and that we'd have a deepened, lasting desire for more of you.

Specifically, I pray for my wife's heart. Let any ongoing temptations that she deals with seem foolish in light of your holiness. Let your ways be delightful in her heart and mind, so much so that she can't get enough of your Word. Hide your Word in her heart so it bears abundant fruit in her actions, attitudes, and desires. Give her tangible, clear opportunities to show kindness to others. Make her aware of the words she says today, and help her understand their effects on those who hear them. Let her thoughts be life-giving, God honoring, and faith filled.

God, thank you for the gift of righteous standing before your throne. It is only by your grace that we can pray to you with confidence and boldness. Holy Spirit, empower us to live righteously and to walk worthy of the calling that we have received (Ephesians 4:1). Stir in us an insatiable appetite for righteousness, and please allow our marriage to flourish as we grow in obedience to you.

In Jesus' name, amen.

Use these pages to journal your thoughts, write your own prayer, or both.

Date ______________

Day 39

That She Would Fix Her Eyes on the Pure

Finally, brothers and sisters, whatever is true, whatever is noble, whatever is right, whatever is pure, whatever is lovely, whatever is admirable—if anything is excellent or praiseworthy—think about such things.

Philippians 4:8 NIV

God, you are pure. You are pure light, pure good, pure love, and so much more. Your every word proves true. You have loved and called us with an unwavering affection (Jeremiah 31:3). As you know, I have not always loved my bride purely. Forgive my wrong motives, transform my heart, and help me to love her as you have loved me (Ephesians 5:25). May I love her purely and earnestly, as you purify my soul and make me obedient to your truth.

Father, today I pray that you'd fix my wife's affections on you and her thoughts on that which is true, excellent, praiseworthy, lovely, and admirable. Holy Spirit, if she begins to look to the right or to the left, graciously remind her of Philippians 4:8. Help her to focus her mind on your truth in every circumstance. Whether she's talking with friends or thinking to herself, re-direct her gaze on all you've commanded. Let it be life to her bones and sweet breath in her lungs.

God, I acknowledge that I don't always lead well in this area. So many times, I let pragmatism and reason coldly determine the emphasis of my words. I repent of the times when I haven't focused on true, noble, and right things—when I have focused on my wisdom instead of yours. Help me to temper my realism and pragmatism with faith and levity.

You are sovereign and in control; I trust you. May my words bring life to my wife, and may my actions reflect all that is admirable, excellent, and praiseworthy. I love you, Lord.

In Jesus' name, amen.

Use these pages to journal your thoughts, write your own prayer, or both. **Date** ______________

Day 40

That She Would Flourish in Every Way

The righteous flourish like the palm tree and grow like a cedar in Lebanon. They are planted in the house of the Lord; they flourish in the courts of our God. They still bear fruit in old age; they are ever full of sap and green

---

Psalm 92:12–14

God, thank you for the gift of prayer. I often take for granted the ability to talk to you and hear from you in return. Grow my faith in this area, and help me to pray continually—as a lifestyle of joy, not a habit of obligation.

Father, as I wrap up this prayer study, I ask that you would cause my beautiful wife to flourish in every way: mentally, physically, spiritually, relationally, and so much more. Plant her as a cedar in Lebanon, in your everlasting courts. If ever she's struggling with anxiety, stress, or depression, lead her beside your still waters and restore her soul (Psalm 23:2–3). If she falls ill, restore her to health quickly. Let her friendships flourish, and give her opportunities and courage to discuss the gospel with her unbelieving friends. I also pray that you'd deepen her friendships with other sisters in the faith. Bring mentors into her life that can provide perspective; align her path with younger women who need to be discipled. Give her every confidence as the wife and mother of our household—let her speak and act with grace and assurance because of who she is in you, Jesus.

Finally, please bless our marriage. Allow our friendship to flourish now and for decades to come. Give us a strong sense of your calling on our lives, and help us to boldly live out the mission you have for us. May the words of our mouths and the works of our hands be pleasing to you! Use us for your glory in our community and beyond. God, I dedicate our marriage to you. Help me to lead well by rejecting passivity and selfishness. Instead, prompt me to serve my family with godly love and righteousness. Thank you for loving me and working in my heart. By your grace, may we both bear fruit now and for many years to come.

I'd be lost without you, Jesus. I love you with all my heart. In your precious name, amen.

Use these pages to journal your thoughts, write your own prayer, or both.

Date ______________

At Journey's End

I hope you've experienced God's grace and faithfulness in new and transformative ways over the past forty days. Spend a few minutes answering the questions below and reflecting on your experience through this book.

How has God moved in your wife's heart over the past forty days? How has he transformed your marriage? Be specific.

Have you changed as a man and as a husband? How?

How has your faith grown? Try to list three specific ways.

Now that you're finished with this book, how will you intentionally pray for your wife?

Knowing what you know now, how will you lead your family by praying for them and with them?

Turn back to page 15 and rate your marriage again. What are the most significant changes?

50 Verses on Prayer

Sometimes we need to be reminded of what the Bible says about prayer. This list of verses is not exhaustive, and each one is part of a greater context. As you read the verses below, note the ones that jump out at you; then read your Bible for surrounding context. Doing so will give you a more thorough understanding of prayer's role and importance in your life.

Rejoice always, pray without ceasing, give thanks in all circumstances; for this is the will of God in Christ Jesus for you.

1 Thessalonians 5:16–18

Do not be anxious about anything, but in everything by prayer and supplication with thanksgiving let your requests be made known to God. And the peace of God, which surpasses all understanding, will guard your hearts and your minds in Christ Jesus.

Philippians 4:6–7

And this is the confidence that we have toward him, that if we ask anything according to his will he hears us.

1 John 5:14

Continue steadfastly in prayer, being watchful in it with thanksgiving.

Colossians 4:2

"Therefore I tell you, whatever you ask in prayer, believe that you have received it, and it will be yours."

Mark 11:24

"Then you will call upon me and come and pray to me, and I will hear you."

Jeremiah 29:12

Rejoice in hope, be patient in tribulation, be constant in prayer.

Romans 12:12

"And when you pray, do not heap up empty phrases as the Gentiles do, for they think that they will be heard for their many words."

Matthew 6:7

The Lord is near to all who call on him,
to all who call on him in truth.

Psalm 145:18

"Call to me and I will answer you, and will tell you great and hidden things that you have not known."

Jeremiah 33:3

"For where two or three are gathered in my name, there am I among them."

Matthew 18:20

Let us then with confidence draw near to the throne of grace, that we may receive mercy and find grace to help in time of need.

Hebrews 4:16

"But when you pray, go into your room and shut the door and pray to your Father who is in secret. And your Father who sees in secret will reward you."

Matthew 6:6

In my distress I called upon the Lord; to my God I cried for help. From his temple he heard my voice, and my cry to him reached his ears.

Psalm 18:6

And if we know that he hears us in whatever we ask, we know that we have the requests that we have asked of him.

1 John 5:15

But let him ask in faith, with no doubting, for the one who doubts is like a wave of the sea that is driven and tossed by the wind.

James 1:6

Therefore, confess your sins to one another and pray for one another, that you may be healed. The prayer of a righteous person has great power as it is working.

James 5:16

"But I say to you who hear, love your enemies, do good to those who hate you, bless those who curse you, pray for those who abuse you."

Luke 6:27–28

About midnight Paul and Silas were praying and singing hymns to God, and the prisoners were listening to them.

Acts 16:25

All these with one accord were devoting themselves to prayer, together with the women and Mary the mother of Jesus, and his brothers.

Acts 1:14

The end of all things is at hand; therefore be self-controlled and sober-minded for the sake of your prayers.

1 Peter 4:7

"You did not choose me, but I chose you and appointed you that you should go and bear fruit and that your fruit should abide, so that whatever you ask the Father in my name, he may give it to you."

John 15:16

"Whatever you ask in my name, this I will do, that the Father may be glorified in the Son."

John 14:13

I cried to him with my mouth,
and high praise was on my tongue.

Psalm 66:17

You desire and do not have, so you murder. You covet and cannot obtain, so you fight and quarrel. You do not have, because you do not ask.

James 4:2

Likewise the Spirit helps us in our weakness. For we do not know what to pray for as we ought, but the Spirit himself intercedes for us with groanings too deep for words.

Romans 8:26

"And whatever you ask in prayer, you will receive, if you have faith."

Matthew 21:22

Out of my distress I called on the Lord;
the Lord answered me and set me free.

Psalm 118:5

For I know that through your prayers and the help of the Spirit of Jesus Christ this will turn out for my deliverance.

Philippians 1:19

O Lord, in the morning you hear my voice;
in the morning I prepare a sacrifice for you and watch.

Psalm 5:3

By day the Lord commands his steadfast love, and at night his song is with me, a prayer to the God of my life.

Psalm 42:8

"If you then, who are evil, know how to give good gifts to your children, how much more will the heavenly Father give the Holy Spirit to those who ask him!"

Luke 11:13

Let the words of my mouth and the meditation of my heart be acceptable in your sight, O Lord, my rock and my redeemer.

Psalm 19:14

Beloved, I pray that all may go well with you and that you may be in good health, as it goes well with your soul.

3 John 2

Hear my prayer, O Lord; give ear to my pleas for mercy!
In your faithfulness answer me, in your righteousness!

Psalm 143:1

"But I say to you, Love your enemies and pray for those who persecute you."

Matthew 5:44

"Father, I desire that they also, whom you have given me, may be with me where I am, to see my glory that you have given me because you loved me before the foundation of the world."

John 17:24

Then after fasting and praying they laid their hands on them and sent them off.

Acts 13:3

And taking the five loaves and the two fish, he looked up to heaven and said a blessing over them. Then he broke the loaves and gave them to the disciples to set before the crowd. And they all ate and were satisfied. And what was left over was picked up, twelve baskets of broken pieces.

Luke 9:16–17

"I made known to them your name, and I will continue to make it known, that the love with which you have loved me may be in them, and I in them."

John 17:26

Arise, O Lord; O God, lift up your hand;
  forget not the afflicted.

Psalm 10:12

For the eyes of the Lord are on the righteous,
  and his ears are open to their prayer.
But the face of the Lord is against those who do evil.

1 Peter 3:12

To you, O God of my fathers, I give thanks and praise, for you have given me wisdom and might, and have now made known to me what we asked of you, for you have made known to us the king's matter.

Daniel 2:23

Is anyone among you sick? Let him call for the elders of the church, and let them pray over him, anointing him with oil in the name of the Lord. And the prayer of faith will save the one who is sick, and the Lord will raise him up. And if he has committed sins, he will be forgiven.

James 5:14–15

"Watch and pray that you may not enter into temptation. The spirit indeed is willing, but the flesh is weak."

Matthew 26:41

"And when you pray, you must not be like the hypocrites. For they love to stand and pray in the synagogues and at the street corners, that they may be seen by others. Truly, I say to you, they have received their reward. But when you pray, go into your room and shut the door and pray to your Father who is in secret. And your Father who sees in secret will reward you. And when you pray, do not heap up empty phrases as the Gentiles do, for they think that they will be heard for their many words. Do not be like them, for your Father knows what you need before you ask him."

Matthew 6:5–8

This poor man cried, and the LORD heard him
  and saved him out of all his troubles.

Psalm 34:6

"Pray then like this: 'Our Father in heaven, hallowed be your name. Your kingdom come, your will be done, on earth as it is in heaven. Give us this day our daily bread, and forgive us our debts, as we also have forgiven our debtors. And lead us not into temptation, but deliver us from evil.'"

Matthew 6:9–13

While they were worshiping the Lord and fasting, the Holy Spirit said, "Set apart for me Barnabas and Saul for the work to which I have called them."

Acts 13:2

Now when all the people were baptized, and when Jesus also had been baptized and was praying, the heavens were opened, and the Holy Spirit descended on him in bodily form, like a dove; and a voice came from heaven, "You are my beloved Son; with you I am well pleased."

Luke 3:21–22

"Turn back, and say to Hezekiah the leader of my people, Thus says the LORD, the God of David your father: I have heard your prayer; I have seen your tears. Behold, I will heal you. On the third day you shall go up to the house of the LORD."

2 Kings 20:5

Additional Resources

You are reading a Fierce Marriage resource. Fierce Marriage exists to point couples to Christ and commission marriages for the gospel. That one mission drives everything we do, this book included. In addition, we produce content daily via our podcast, blog, and on social media.

The Fierce Marriage Podcast

Listen in every week as Ryan and Selena discuss modern marriage issues in light of the gospel. Subscribe and listen on iTunes, Spotify, or anywhere else podcasts are found.

Find Us Online

Website: FierceMarriage.com
Email: FierceMarriage.com/List
Facebook: /FierceMarriage
Instagram: @FierceMarriage
YouTube: /FierceMarriage
Twitter: @FierceMarriage

Recommended Books

For a list of books we love and recommend, visit FierceMarriage.com/Resources.

Share This Book with a Friend

If you'd like to share this book with a friend, please direct them to 40Prayers.com.

Share an Image

Snap a picture of you and your spouse and share it using our hashtags, #40Prayers and #FierceMarriage. We'd love to see your faces and see how our resources are helping you!

Do You Have Feedback or a Story?

If this book has helped you, please share your story with us. If we can improve or fix anything about this resource, please let us know by sending an email to care@fiercemarriage.com.

Want to Leave a Review?

If you've enjoyed this book, we'd be honored if you wrote an honest review wherever you purchased your copy (on our website, Amazon.com, or elsewhere). Make sure to share how God is working in your marriage. You never know who might read it and be encouraged.

Group Study Leaders

If you would like to lead a small group based on this book, bulk discounts are available (8+ copies). Please email details to care@fiercemarriage.com and someone will be in touch.

Speaking Requests

Ryan and Selena are happy to work alongside churches and event organizers to bring gospel-centered hope and help to couples around the world through relatable teaching.

For speaking inquiries, visit FierceMarriage.com/Speaking.

ALSO AVAILABLE

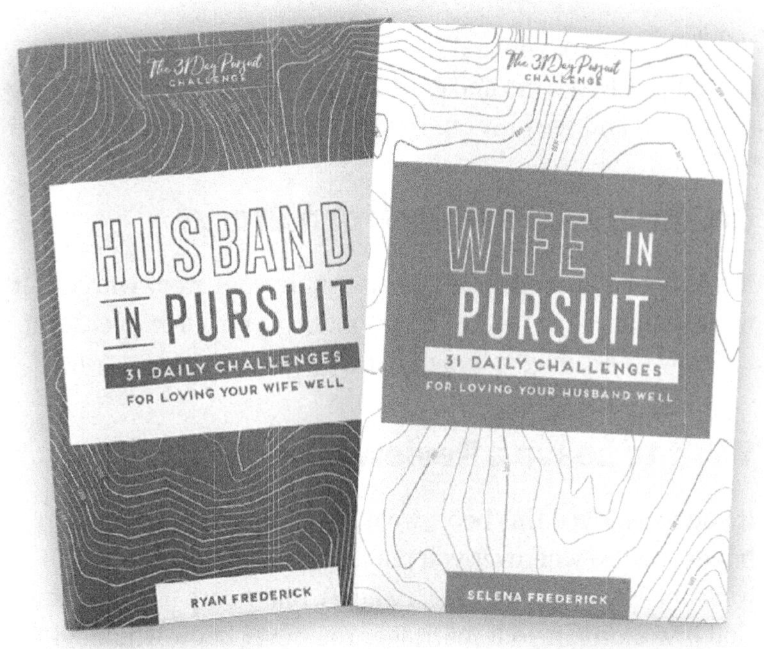

Take the 31-Day Pursuit Challenge

Husband in Pursuit and *Wife in Pursuit* offer a gospel-centered path for couples who want to learn to creatively love each other as Christ has loved them. Over thirty-one days, you and your wife will dive into God's Word, rediscover how Christ has pursued you, and take intentional action to pursue each other.

Take the 31-Day Pursuit Challenge together.

Learn more at **31DayPursuit.com**

ALSO AVAILABLE

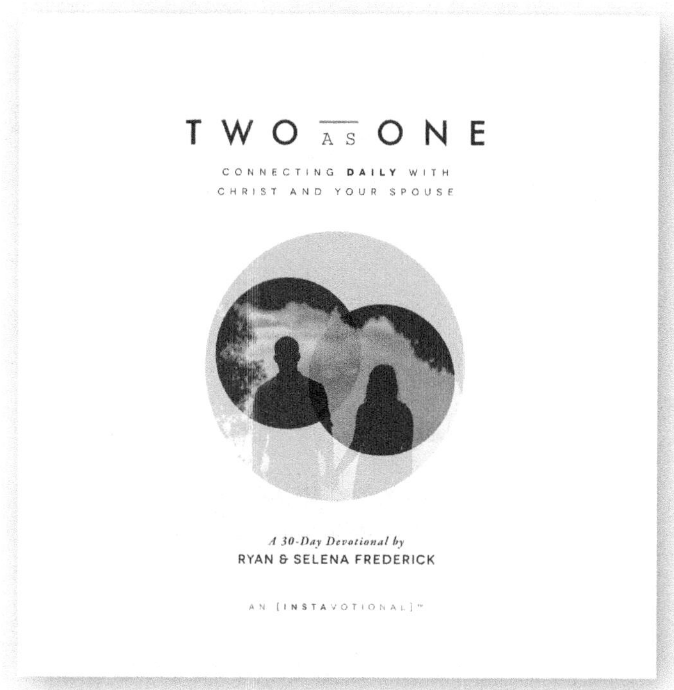

A 30-Day Couple's Devotional

Draw closer to God and your wife through thirty daily devotions, each one brought to life with imagery and practical application.

Each day starts with an image/quote combination designed to inspire and stimulate conversation. Explore passages of the Bible, connect the gospel to real challenges, and pray alongside your wife.

Learn more at **TwoAsOne.org**

Pray without ceasing.

1 Thessalonians 5:17

Made in the USA
Coppell, TX
20 March 2021

52056048R10108